S0-AJO-741

THE
PRONGHORN

by Iona Seibert Hiser

Illustrated by Carol Rogers

Steck-Vaughn Company
An Intext Publisher
Austin, Texas

Library of Congress Cataloging in Publication Data

Hiser, Iona Seibert.
  The pronghorn.

  SUMMARY: Describes briefly the habits and characteristics of the endangered pronghorn antelope and its subspecies.

  1. Pronghorn antelope—Juvenile literature. 2. Rare animals—Juvenile literature. [1. Pronghorn antelope. 2. Animals, Rare] I. Rogers, Carol, illus. II. Title.

QL737.U53H57   599'.7358   72-5563
ISBN 0-8114-7751-7

Introduction

North America's pronghorn, prongbuck, or pronghorn antelope is not a true antelope. The name "pronghorn antelope" probably originated from the Spaniards who thought the pronghorn on this continent belonged to the same family as the antelopes in Africa and Asia. They called the swiftly running animal "verendo," antelope. But pronghorns are not closely related to antelopes of the Old World.

The Pronghorn

Order: Artiodactyla (are-dee-uh-dak-tul-uh)
Family: Antilocapridae (an-tuli-low-cap ruh dee),
        Pronghorns are the only surviving members of this family.
Genus: Antilocapra americana

1

The Pronghorns' Family

Pronghorns are true North Americans
that developed on this continent. But they
are grouped in an order of even-toed,
hoofed mammals.

Giraffe

Bactrian Camel

Red Deer

Gray Duiker
(die-kur)

Collared
Peccary

Common
Hippopotamus

Wild Boar

Lesser Malay Chevrotain
(shev-ruh-tan)

Topi

Giant Sable

Oryx

American Buffalo (Bison)

Bighorn Sheep

Cow

Common Goat

True antelopes are members of the Bovidae (<u>bov</u>-vuh-dee) family, including cattle, sheep, goats, and buffaloes.

There are a number of subspecies of the Antilocapra americana, all very similar in appearance. They are named according to the area in which they are found.

Although the pronghorn can be found in much of its former range, some areas show a decrease in numbers.

Former Range of the Pronghorn

4

By the first quarter of this century, pronghorns had become very scarce. But conservation practices have resulted in increased populations for the American and Mexican pronghorns.

However, the peninsular pronghorns found in Baja California, Mexico, are feared to be extinct. And the Sonoran pronghorns found in Sonora, Mexico, and our Sonoran desert are considered endangered animals. Distribution formerly extended from the desert plains of central western Sonora, north to southern Arizona. Now the Sonoran pronghorn can be found in the United States only in a limited portion of the Cabeza Prieta Game Range and the Organ Pipe Cactus National Monument, Arizona. Reduced in range and numbers, this small, pale pronghorn must depend upon international cooperation for survival.

A Antilocapra americana americana
B Antilocapra americana mexicana
C Antilocapra americana oregona
D Antilocapra americana peninsularis
    (puh-nin-suh-lare-is)
E Antilocapra americana sonoriensis
    (sun-nor-ee-en-sis)

What Pronghorns Look Like

When startled or curious, the pronghorn has a habit of stopping its cud chewing, placing the lower jaw off to one side. This gives its face a comical misshapen look.

The showy markings; the tan, white, and black coloring; and the proudly carried black horns make pronghorns some of our most beautiful animals. The broken color pattern serves as a camouflage (<u>kam</u>-uh-flahzh) and makes the animals difficult to distinguish from their surroundings.

Buck's Weight—100 pounds up to 125 pounds
Height—4 feet to 4½ feet, 3 feet at shoulder
Length—about 5 feet
Females are about 10 percent smaller than males.

American Saddle Horse

The two-toed feet have sharp, pointed hoofs that make good digging tools. Hoofs have padding that cushions the feet and keeps them from becoming sore.

The buck's face is darker than the doe's and has a conspicuous black spot on each side of the lower jaw. Dark-lashed black eyes, well protected in deep sockets, are large and have an exceptionally wide range of vision. The pronghorn's sight is believed to be about 8 times stronger than man's.

Horns of the female are smaller and less forked than the male's.

Large, pointed ears can be moved to catch warning sounds from any direction.

The short, brown tail fits neatly into a groove or is carried horizontally.

7

The Pelage

Separate hairs of the coarse, hairy coat are filled with spongy material containing air cells which act as an insulator and protect the animal against heat and cold. When exposed to broiling desert sun, pronghorns can use muscles attached to the skin and raise the hairs, or pelage (pel-ij), thus letting cooling breezes through.

On high mountain plateaus where weather is often cold, the sparse wool scattered through the body hair is not much protection. But pronghorns keep warm by pulling down their air-filled hairs to overlap, thus forming a smooth insulating blanket.

Black-tipped hairs, 3 to 4 inches long, are raised as a first sign of fear or used as a display during courtship.

Effective Signaling Devices

With powerful vision, pronghorns can spot small, moving objects miles away, easily detecting lurking enemies. When suspicious, the pronghorn stands with raised head, staring intently. If there is real danger, the animal utters a loud snort and immediately signals other members of the herd by raising the hairs in the large, white patch on its rump which forms a circle called a "rosette." This rosette has sparkling white hairs ranging in length from almost 4 inches at the top to less than 2 inches lower down.

Hairs are so pithy that they are very brittle and break easily. Thus the hide is of no value as a rug or robe.

Normally, these hairs lie flat, pointing backward. But during fright, special muscles contract and instantly raise the hairs to form a bristly, fanlike circle of brilliant white easily seen for miles. As the hair is raised, the resulting flash is much like that of a mirror used to send messages by reflecting the sun's rays. Hence, pronghorns are sometimes called "heliographers" (hee-lee-<u>og</u>-graf-ers), a term used to describe those who signal by means of the rays of the sun.

When the rosette is erected, two of the animal's musk glands located on the rump automatically open and send out a strong musky odor so intense that man can detect it from hundreds of feet away. Pronghorns can smell it much farther. The scent warns others of danger and tells them the sender is a friend.

When nearby pronghorns notice the signals, they quickly raise their rosettes, opening the musk glands, thus dispatching the twin messages even farther. After the warning, the various groups race to one spot as if prearranged and then string out in a single file to flee at speeds up to 60 miles an hour. Usually the line is led by a mature doe, while a fine buck—probably herd boss— follows at the rear as guard.

Home of the Pronghorn

The fastest runner of North America's hoofed mammals, the pronghorn skims over wide-open spaces. The animal does not like heavily forested country.

In early times, pronghorns traveled in vast herds over grassy plains and rolling foothill country west of the Mississippi River. But as civilization moved westward, bringing herds of domestic animals and fences, the pronghorns gradually were forced off the Great Plains and into areas with more trees.

Winter on the Plains

Since pronghorns thrive in both hot and cold climates, they make no great migrations. But they do drift from one feeding ground to another with change of the season or for a better supply of food. Usually they prefer cooler highlands during summer and lower, warmer places in winter.

Summer on Slopes and High Plateaus

Food of the Pronghorn

Feeding on various grasses, shrubby plants, and wild flowers, the graceful animals eat daintily, not trampling and ruining growth they do not want.

Grasses and
Wild Flowers

Common
White
Daisy

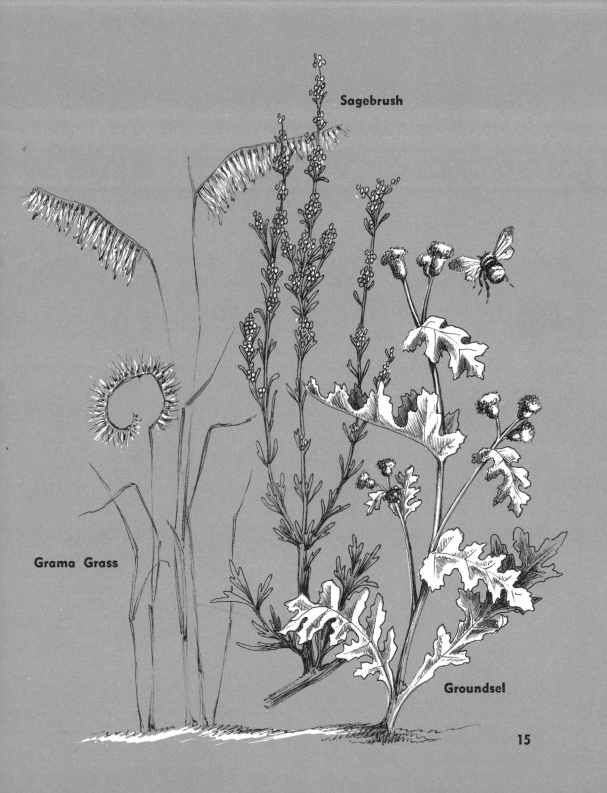

Sagebrush

Grama Grass

Groundsel

15

Unique Horns

Both males and females have horns. The horns of the doe usually are much shorter than those of the male. The bucks' horns average a length of about 13 inches along the outer side of the curve.

This headgear is different from that of any other animal. Cattle, sheep, and goats have hollow horns that are never shed. Deer grow solid antlers that are shed and renewed yearly. Giraffe horns, covered with soft, hairy skin, are never dropped.

Longhorn

Bighorn Sheep

Common Goat

The pronghorn has a special combination. From its head, just above the eyes, grow permanent bony horn cores. Over these cores grow hollow horns with one prong. The horns fit over the cores much as a leather sheath encases a hunting knife.

Once a year these hollow sheaths are shed. New growth starts before the old horns are dropped. Pressure from within loosens and finally sheds the old sheaths. This leaves the solid cores partly exposed until the new horns finish growing.

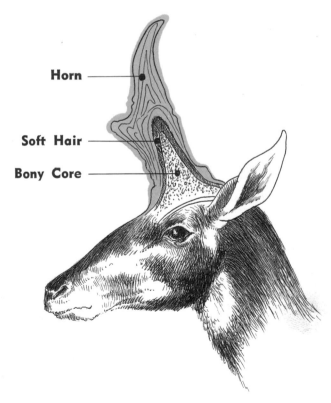

Horn

Soft Hair

Bony Core

Family Life and Habits

Pronghorns like companionship. They
live in groups of varying sizes as they
feed and roam from one water hole to
another. As fall approaches, the mature
bucks become restless and start looking
for mates. Each tries to collect a few
does. To attract the opposite sex, the
bucks stage quite a show.

To begin, one will stand with head hung
low, as if ill. Then suddenly his showy
white rosette is expanded to its full
extent, spreading beyond the normal body
line by several inches. The sparkling
hairs begin to wave in a continuous
movement as they are raised and lowered.
To add drama, the long, black hairs of
the mane and those above the tail are
also raised. As a final flourish, the buck
may abruptly give a stiff-legged jump to
one side, as if avoiding some sudden
danger.

Fights sometimes occur. Bulging their eyes ferociously, two bucks occasionally battle so violently that one is killed. Defeated warriors are driven from the herd until the mating season is over. Later, after the horns are shed in October and November and the conquering males are not so quarrelsome, the banished are permitted to return.

About 8 months after the mating, the kids, sometimes called "fawns," are born. During the fawning period, the old bucks usually live as "bachelors," leaving yearlings and mothers with young to wander in groups by themselves.

The mother has no nest or den. She goes off by herself, but not too far from the others, to give birth. After the young, usually twins, have been licked clean, they have no odor. This helps to keep predators from finding and killing them.

Rippling hair also helps to camouflage the young and to protect them from enemies.

For the first week or so, fawns spend much time flattened on the ground, blending with and fading into their surroundings of earth, rock, and shadow so completely they are almost impossible to see from even a short distance.

The mother stations twins in separate locations. To avoid attracting an enemy's attention to the babies, she stays at quite a distance from both, vigilantly keeping watch. Occasionally she goes to nurse them.

If her young are threatened by predators, the mother swiftly comes to the rescue, fighting valiantly with horns and sharp hoofs. Should the attacker be too large or ferocious, she instinctively tries to lure the enemy away by offering herself as a tempting bait.

The mother takes the young and rejoins the band soon after the kids are about one week old, at which time fawns can run swiftly themselves—as fast as 25 miles an hour, if necessary.

Pronghorns employ "baby sitters." One
doe will care for a group of kids while
their mothers wander off to feed or rest.
When lying down, pronghorns usually
face in different directions to more easily
see possible danger.

Enemies

Wolves, coyotes, bobcats, and
occasionally mountain lions are predators.
Bears, foxes, and eagles can kill or badly
injure fawns. Disease, too, often attacks
pronghorns and causes death. Sheep may
destroy their winter range, and deep snows
can prevent them from foraging.

Mountain Lion

Bobcat

Bear

Eagles

Sheep

Coyote

Fox

Wolf

25

Curiosity

Pronghorns possess enormous curiosity which often leads them into trouble. They seem compelled to investigate carefully anything unusual. A fluttering movement, a new object, even a desert "dust devil" arouses their interest. If possible trouble is spotted, the animals move forward cautiously in a stiff manner, running swiftly away if threatened.

Any great activity of men or machines draws their attention. Pronghorns have been known to watch for hours the construction work on the site of a new highway.

Pronghorns at Play

Speed not only is the pronghorns' protection but also appears to give the animals pleasure. They apparently take satisfaction in outracing moving objects, and they seem to instinctively try to prevent anything from catching up with them or passing them while running. Sometimes they speed alongside a car for some distance, then suddenly with an explosive burst of extra energy, tear across the road in front of the automobile.

Pronghorns can travel easily at 35 to 40 miles an hour and, when threatened, race away in very smooth running strides at higher speeds. They do not bound as sheep, and they are not good at high jumping. However, while traveling at top speed they can leap a span of quite a long distance.

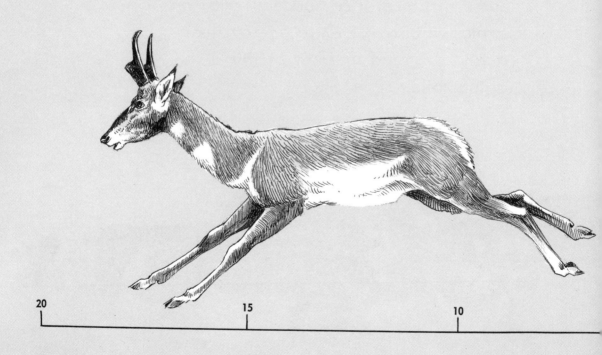

20   15   10

Aside from love of running, adults appear quite dignified. But kids are very playful. They form a line of 6 or 7 and together sweep off across the country in a huge circle. When tired of that, they may start a game of hopping from the back of one mother to another as the patient does lie resting.

5   0

At one time, man was the pronghorn's worst enemy, but as a result of carefully planned conservation practices, the pronghorn population has increased. Controlled hunting provides sport, trophy, and meat. But the pronghorn, like other forms of wildlife, may face a crisis: the destruction of its natural environment.

Special efforts are needed to preserve the environment, protecting all of earth's creatures as well as safeguarding the existence of those graceful animals, the pronghorns. And also a matter of much concern is the rescue of those subspecies in danger. If it is not too late, the pronghorn in Baja California and the pale little pronghorn of our southwestern Sonoran desert may be rescued.